BRING ME OUT

TABLE OF CONTENTS

DEDICATION

First, I dedicate this book to my Father Yahweh, to my King Yeshua, and to my Teacher and Friend the Holy Spirit. You rescued me from the darkness I created and walked me out step by step. Every page in this book is evidence of Your mercy, Your deliverance, and Your unfailing love. All glory forever belongs to You.

I dedicate this also to my wife, April—the woman who prayed for me when I didn't know how to pray for myself; who fought for me when I was ready to quit; who forgave me when I didn't deserve forgiveness; and who stayed when everything in our story said she should leave. Thank you for loving me while God was still teaching me how to be a husband, a man of God, and a father. And to my step-kids, thank you for continuing to be there and caring for me while I learned how to be the stepdad you deserved. You are proof of God's grace in my life.

I dedicate this to my family—those who loved me while I was lost, addicted, and broken, and those who stood by me when I came home a new man, learning to walk with Jesus and rebuild my life. Your patience and love carried me farther than you realize.

I also want to honor Prophet Bobby Conner, who obeyed the Lord to speak a word over my life that unlocked the author inside of me. Your obedience helped open a doorway I didn't know existed.

And to my spiritual mother and father, thank you for reading this manuscript before its release, for your encouragement, your discernment, and your support as I stepped into this assignment. Your covering and your wisdom have shaped my walk more than you know.

Finally, I dedicate this book to every person who has ever felt trapped, ashamed, overlooked, or too far gone to change. If God could bring me out, He can bring you out too. This book is not just my story—it's an invitation to your freedom.

PASS IT ON

If this book helps you in any way, I ask you for one simple favor...

Pass it on.

Buy another copy.
Give it to someone who needs hope, freedom, or a fresh start.

Please consider helping someone else by sharing it forward.

You are part of this mission now.
Together, we can spread the message of Jesus — one life at a time.

BORN INTO THE FIRE

Chapter 1

Pop. Pop. Pop. Shots rang out, just missing the tail end of a blacked-out BMW—the one my two homies and I had just jumped into. Moments earlier, we thought it was a great idea to collect on an unpaid debt from a bad dope deal. What we didn't know was that the guy we were trying to tax was part of one of the biggest gangs in Ogden—the 18th Streeters. We showed up at the apartment thinking we were big, bad, and untouchable. Knocked on the door. No answer. But as we walked away, we realized the situation was far from over. The guy we were after wasn't hiding—he was already in the parking lot. And he wasn't alone. He had about ten people with him. Ten against three. Not great odds. But really, it was my homie's bad deal, not ours. Did we really have to fight an entire gang for him?

Thankfully, there's still some kind of twisted honor code in the hood. Instead of all-out war, my homie and the guy went at it one-on-one. My homie—big dude, bigger attitude—stomped him into the pavement. And that's when the hornet's nest broke loose. The rest of them weren't about to stand by and let their boy take that alone. Suddenly, we had a full-on mob coming for us. That's when we ran for the BMW. We had no idea we were about to get shot at.

That was just one of many times I put myself in a place I never should have been. This story really begins in 1982, when I decided to jump out of my mother's womb. My mom was a beautiful brunette with two sisters, raised by a single mother. Her dad—my grandpa—passed away young, so I never met him. Compared to her sisters, my mom was the rebellious one. She loved to party, and because of that, I exist. She wasn't sure who my father was. I was the result of a one-night stand. I didn't know my dad's name until I was 38—but that's a story for a different book.

I was born in Ogden, Utah. Some of you might be thinking, *Where's that?* It's next to Arizona and Wyoming—you know, the *Mormon* state. If you don't know what a Mormon is, they're members of the Church of Jesus Christ of Latter-day Saints, founded by Joseph Smith in 1830. I'm not Mormon. Even though I have family, friends, and coworkers who are, and I love them dearly, I just don't agree with their beliefs.

Ogden wasn't always the quiet, small-town people might imagine. It was settled by Mormon pioneers in 1850, but when the railroad came through, it became a breeding ground for liquor, gambling, and violence. Even Al Capone himself passed through in the 1920s and said Ogden was too wild for him. Despite all that, the city is surrounded by beauty—mountains, trees, and some pretty interesting characters.

I'm one of them.

I don't remember much of my early years, but I know we lived in a trailer park at first—the same one I'd find myself back in at age 30, surrounded by the FBI and local task force looking to arrest me. By the time I was two, my mom had managed to get us into a better part of town—Ron Claire, almost North Ogden. But she was a bartender, which meant I spent a lot of time at my grandma's while she worked. My first memories of a bar are barely being able to see over the counter, looking at my mom as she poured drinks. The devil had already played his hand, using her lifestyle against both of us.

My grandma was your average, sweet American grandma. I loved being with her—she took me to the mall, bought me toys, and took me to the movies. But she had her own flaws. I remember walking through stores with her, watching her slip things into her purse. So, on one hand, I had my mom—drinking, partying, and working late nights at the bar. On the other, I had my grandma—who loved me, spoiled me, but also had no problem shoplifting.

I remember that my grandma was somewhat religious. I didn't really understand what that meant back then—I just remember Mormon women coming to the house, reading from the Book of Mormon. I didn't know who God was yet, or even what religion really was. What stood out to me the most about being at my grandma's house wasn't religion, it was the freedom. I loved how free I felt there, even though that freedom eventually led me to a group of neighborhood kids who weren't exactly the best influence.

There were about ten of us, running around pretending to be soldiers, Native Americans, and mostly—ninjas. But we didn't just play dress-up. We ordered ninja suits and stars from magazines, snuck out at night, and did things no kids should be doing—throwing rocks through windows, setting dummies in the road to make cars swerve, then pelting them with rocks. That was my life between ages seven and eleven. We also did things kids shouldn't do. Sexual things.

Mainly because of what we were exposed to—MTV, movies filled with half-naked women, and no parental supervision.

It also didn't help that the first time I saw porn was in my mother's closet while playing hide-and-seek. I found a stash of magazines with naked men in them.

Then, at eleven, my world shifted. My grandma had a stroke and passed away. Everything changed. That group of boys I ran with started drifting apart. Some of us kept walking the road of darkness. Some found the straight and narrow. The last time my mom let me stay over at one of my old friends' houses, we got caught throwing rocks at cars. That was it—she put an end to that crew. After that I tried to do the "right" thing—I got baptized into the Mormon church. I didn't fully understand it, but I thought it would honor my grandma. I met with missionaries, learned about the Book of Mormon, and took the plunge.

But that didn't change who I was.

Around that time, one of my mom's ex-boyfriends resurfaced. His parents had recently passed away, and with nowhere else to go, he moved in with us—bringing his son and daughter along. Almost overnight, they became like siblings to me. For the first time, I had what felt like a real brother and sister. But their dad wasn't exactly a role model. He was deep into the drug game, and it wasn't long before he ended up in prison.

Even after he was gone, his kids remained a big part of my life. We spent our days playing video games, running around dressed as ninjas, and getting into things we had no business being involved in. Left to our own devices, we made our own rules. We stole pot from my mom, smoked it while she was at work, and did whatever we could get away with. We were just kids, but the world we were growing up in was shaping us fast. Eventually, their dad got out and moved in with his new girlfriend. They left, and from that point on, I barely saw them.

Over time, my bond with my little brother remained, but we were both on the same self-destructive path. He's still caught up in that same crazy lifestyle, and I pray that one day he finds his way out. My sister, on the other hand, helped me in ways I'll never be able to repay. She was always there for me, but I know I hurt her with some of my actions when her dad passed away. Because of that, she hasn't spoken to me in years. If either of you ever read this, I love you dearly. I hope one day we can reconcile our differences.

I don't want to paint my childhood as completely terrible. My mom did her best. She was a single mom who pushed through college while raising me, eventually earning her bachelor's degree in business. Despite everything, I have good memories—trips to Yellowstone, SeaWorld, and Disneyland with my grandma and mom. Camping and boating trips, even if they involved drinking and drugs. Through it all, my mom loved me fiercely. She just had her own demons. And by the time I was old enough to understand what was happening, I had already let my own demons in, too.

A TEENAGE WARZONE

Chapter 2

Alright, some of you might be wondering—wasn't this book supposed to be about how God can bring me out of the places I put myself into? And it is. But before I can show you how He does that, I must take you through a lifetime of bad choices—places I put myself into—so you can truly understand the journey. Stick with me, because I promise, by the time you finish this book, your life will change.

Now, let's dive into the teenage years—some parents' nightmare. It's that stage where it seems like a kid's mind is disconnected from reality, lost in physical, mental, and even spiritual changes. Looking back, I barely remember turning 13, but I do remember stepping into middle school and all the chaos that came with it.

You can probably guess the kind of crowd I started hanging out with. Growing up listening to MTV and gangster rap—Easy-E, Tupac, Dr. Dre, and Snoop

Dogg—it was no surprise I gravitated toward the so-called "gangsters." I fell in with a crew that I thought was cool, and while they accepted me, they also picked on me for being the nerdy white kid. But in middle school, you fit in wherever you can, and for me, that was with the troublemakers.

We didn't hang out much outside of school, though, since we lived in different areas. So, outside of school, I was mostly a loner. Academically, I was okay—I excelled in math and art, but I was terrible at reading, spelling, and English. Cheating got me through most English tests and reports. I never had a girlfriend in middle school—chubby white wannabe gang-sters weren't exactly in high demand.

Despite my crowd, I did make one real friend. We spent a lot of time together, even working with his dad trimming trees for extra cash. Our nights were filled with watching *Beavis and Butthead* and prank-calling girls. But that friendship ended when he got into meth.

That experience made me swear off meth, though I had already experimented with weed and alcohol.

Middle school flew by. By the summer I turned 14, I was working full-time, first in a youth program helping clean up campgrounds, then as a school janitor. That job helped me contribute financially at home and gave me a sense of responsibility. By high school, I had lost some weight, gotten taller, and started catching the attention of girls—and noticing them more, too.

Despite my new look, my crowd didn't change. I stuck with the gangsters and even started hanging out with the skater kids, most of whom had rough home lives or were deep into drugs.

I didn't ditch school much. Even while running with troublemakers, I managed to stay out of trouble— at least in front of authority figures. My mom called me her "little angel," but I was far from it. Behind the scenes, I was battling depression, anxiety, and constant lying. I remember my mom yelling at me, "Stop lying, boy!" and me swearing I wasn't.

Teenagers think they're so smart, but looking back, I see how much I was deceiving myself.

At 16, I got my first car—an '88 Honda Civic. It already had nice rims, so I lowered it and installed a loud stereo system. Feeling like a big shot, I started my own car club, *Unseen Talent.* It was a cheesy name, but my leadership skills were already surfacing. We grew to about 15 members, all with different rides and backgrounds. That car got me into places I should've never been—like racing in the mall parking lot, tearing up Washington Blvd., and constantly getting pulled over for speeding, loitering, or having modified parts.

At 17, I had my first serious girlfriend—a beautiful Mexican girl from school. Since my mom worked a lot, my house became our private getaway, where we did things we shouldn't have. My mom never emphasized waiting for marriage; in fact, she bought me my first condoms and Playboy magazine. My girlfriend came from a similar background, so our relationship was doomed from the start.

It all fell apart when I gave a drunk girl a ride home from a party. We stopped at a gas station, and she started crawling all over me. My girlfriend's friends saw and reported back to her, ending our relationship in a mess. If she ever reads this, I apologize and I hope you can forgive me. Back then, I had no concept of loyalty, which led to a string of disastrous relationships down the road.

As high school continued, my choices worsened. I got involved with worse crowds and used my free time recklessly. In chemistry class, a couple of us thought it'd be a great idea to smoke weed in the back of the room while the teacher was out. Foolish teenagers always think they won't get caught—of course, we did.

Despite everything, I somehow managed to graduate—mostly because my mom convinced my 12th grade English teacher to change my failing grade to a passing one. In my senior year, I attended a technical school and learned bricklaying, landing a job as a hod tender right after graduation.

But from 18 to 19, my life took a sharp turn downhill. I dove headfirst into partying—ecstasy, cocaine, weed, opium—pretty much anything except meth. My new girlfriend, however, was deep in it, along with her siblings. I still swore I'd never touch meth, remembering how it stole my middle school friend. But one night at a party, curiosity got the best of me, and I tried it for the first time. That first hit was awful. I didn't even want to do it again. But I did. My girlfriend was my perfect source, and most of my homies were selling it.

My life spiraled into addiction, crime, and desperation. I started stealing car stereos, shoplifting high-end clothes, and doing whatever I could to get more meth. I got arrested for the first time at 19 for shoplifting. Before I knew it, I was a full-blown addict, running with dealers, staying up for weeks at a time.

My weight dropped to 120 pounds, and my girlfriend looked like something out of a National Geographic special. My mom hated meth heads, so we avoided my home, crashing in my car or dope houses.

That relationship ended in screaming matches and violence—it wasn't love, just a chemical romance. From there, I just kept running the streets, spiraling into a life of homelessness, crime, and drugs.

If you're reading this and thinking,

This doesn't apply to me—I had a perfect upbringing,

GOOD—keep reading.

RUNNING IN THE DARKNESS

Chapter 3

My teenage years were a crash course in bad decisions, rebellion, and self-destruction. And yet, my story doesn't end there. By the time I turned 21, I was already running the streets with more dope than water. Home had become just a pit stop—when I went back, my mom and I would argue constantly. She'd tell me to get my life together, but in my eyes, she was just a hypocrite. She drank and partied just as much as anyone else. I still wasn't a big drinker, but now that I was legal, the doors to nightclubs and bars swung wide open. It was a whole new world of partying that I had yet to experience, at least legally.

The world has a monopoly on alcohol, making it seem harmless just because it's legal. And now, we see other drugs becoming legal too. In reality, it's just a demonic open door—one I walked right through without hesitation.

I thought I was having the time of my life, but all it really brought was sickness, pain, and drama. It only made it harder to hold down a job. I remember going to the club every single night for two weeks straight. Pretty pathetic, right? What kind of club even stays open Sunday through Wednesday? But strip clubs, bars, and dance clubs don't care. That's how they make their money.

During this time, I did spend more time at home. I drank with my mom, smoked weed with her, and, as always, we ended up arguing. It gave me an excuse to run back to the streets, back to tweaking out and selling drugs. My mom was really sick by then—she had been getting worse since I was 18. Doctor after doctor tried to figure out what was wrong, but I don't know how honest she was with them. What I did know was that she was taking more pills, drinking more, and constantly stressing about me. I'm sure my reckless lifestyle only made things worse for her. One year, I completely forgot my mom's birthday. I felt horrible, but when you're high and full of demons, it doesn't seem to matter much.

Then one night, while installing a car stereo, I got a phone call from her. She was at the hospital, saying she wasn't going to make it. The last time I saw her, she already looked bad. She had told me she had cirrhosis of the liver—her skin and eyes were completely yellow. But I was in denial. Instead of rushing to see her, I chose to get high.

That phone call was short. I mostly ignored what she was saying. It was the last time I would ever hear my mother's voice. And I lied. I told her I was coming to see her, but I never did.

The next phone call came the day before Mother's Day. It was from my mom's friend. My mom had chosen to go home to die. She passed away there, alone. When I got the call, I threw my phone in anger—I swore it shattered to pieces. But when I went inside, my brother handed it back to me, completely intact. I called my mom's friend back and said I was coming.

When I arrived at the house, a police officer and my mom's friend were waiting. They were either waiting for an ambulance or the morgue—I can't even remember. My mom had already been dead for a couple of days. Our dogs had been trapped inside the house with her. They let me go in to see her. Her eyes were open; her body was cold and stiff. I tried to do what they do in movies—to close her eyes—but it didn't work. I held her and cried, apologizing for everything.

If you're reading this, please—if you still have your loved ones, no matter what you're going through, don't ignore them. Love them. Do your best, even if you're high, depressed, or struggling. No matter how hard it seems, just love them while you can. Because you never know when the last phone call will come. If you can, call them right now and tell them you love them.

If you're reading this and I know you personally,

I love you.

From the time I was 20 to 22, I met a family that became like my own. The mother treated me like a son, and her kids felt like my siblings. I spent a lot of time at their house because I could get high there without judgment. They used to call me 'the guy behind the couch' because I would always fall asleep back there.

When my mom passed away, I moved in with them, and they became even more of a family to me. Around that time, I started dating one of their cousins. It was a little weird since her family was like my family, but we weren't blood related. She had a young son and was buying a house with her mom. We didn't exactly 'date'—it was more like me asking her to hang out while I got high and sold drugs.

Honestly, I have no idea why she fell in love with me. We never even talked about it. Maybe she saw the good in me that I couldn't see in myself. It was my first serious relationship since high school, but I wasn't any kind of man—not one worthy of being a stepfather.

Her son had already been abandoned by his real dad, who chose prison and drugs over raising his child. And here I was, thinking I was better than him. But really, I was just another doper low life.

This relationship lasted a few years. She put up with a lot, but eventually, she had enough. Our breakup was ugly and painful for both of us. If you're reading this and you know who you are, I apologize for everything I put you and your family through. I hope that you can truly forgive me. May you and your family be blessed.

During that time, I caught my first felonies. Even though I was drinking and getting high the whole time, I still managed to complete probation. After the breakup I completely spiraled out of control. Throughout my mid-20s, I was arrested multiple times—charges ranging from theft to driving on a revoked license to drug dealing, and possession of drugs and paraphernalia. I dated several women, but none of the relationships worked because they were all built on addiction.

I even went through drug court, AA, and NA pro-
grams, which helped me stay sober for a while—mainly
from meth—but none of them brought lasting freedom.

By the end of my 20s, I remember my friend driving me to California to scatter my mom's ashes into the
ocean. On our way back, we stopped in Vegas. We took
mushrooms and smoked meth, partying all night. After that, things just kept getting worse.

I found myself in places flooded with dope—and
even witches. Yes, literal witches practicing voodoo and
dark rituals. At that point, I didn't know God at all. My
life was so lost and filled with darkness that I had created
my own version of God.

Eventually, I caught a one-to-fifteen-year charge
for drug dealing. I had been set up by a so-called friend,
and I knew prison was inevitable. I went completely off
the rails, stealing mail, checks, identities—committing
fraud like crazy.

But this would all lead to my freedom.

THE RESCUE

Chapter 4

This chapter is where everything truly begins to shift. Salvation starts here. If you don't know God yet, this chapter will be the moment that changes everything.

The last months of my twenties and the first few of my thirties were a complete blur of destruction. I had started dating the last girlfriend I would ever get high with. We were deep in it—selling drugs, using meth, committing fraud, and worse. We thought we were untouchable. But the truth is, we were walking straight into a trap of our own making.

On April 27, 2012, it all came crashing down. The trailer park where we were staying was surrounded. The FBI and a local task force had been quietly building a case against us, and that day, the hammer fell.

They kicked in the door.

Just like that, it was over. But that moment wasn't just an arrest, it was a rescue. God wasn't going to let me die in my sin. He had other plans.

This time, I didn't cry out to God in desperation like I had with previous arrests. I didn't beg for help. I didn't even say His name. I was silent. Not because I didn't need Him, but because I didn't know Him. I only knew darkness—witchcraft, demons, and deception. I was surrounded by spiritual bondage, and I didn't even realize how deep it ran.

Two weeks into jail, a fellow inmate invited me to a Bible study. Nothing fancy—just a few guys at a cold metal table in the pod after breakfast. The man who led it was a rough, gangster type, but he spoke about Jesus with power and authority. Something in me stirred. We opened the Bible to the book of John and read about Jesus being the Light of the world. That's when it happened—something shifted inside me.

I heard God speak to my heart: *"It's going to be okay, son. I will walk through this with you, step by step."*

Not long after that, I prayed a real prayer: *"Jesus, if You're real, show me."*

And He answered.

He began to speak to me—through the Bible, through prayer, and through people. I started to understand who Jesus really was—not the Jesus of tradition or religion, but the living, breathing Son of God. The One who came for the broken. The One who came for me.

I remember walking around in the pod, talking to the Christian brother who had invited me to the Bible study. I asked him, "What's a Christian?" and he said, "It's someone who confesses Jesus as their Lord and believes in their heart that God raised Him from the dead. That's when you become a Christ follower—a Christian." That's when I said yes to Jesus.

I spent the next four and a half years locked up. The first 18 months were just waiting to be sentenced. During that time, I went to every religious service I could. I was hungry.

I devoured the New Testament over and over. I even read parts of the Book of Mormon—trying to figure out who Jesus really was. I was desperate for the Truth. Even though I had heard His voice, I still had a lot of misunderstandings. I didn't know what it meant to truly follow Christ, to be a "Christian" but I was ready to learn.

From the beginning, I felt God saying He had a purpose for me, that I would one day lead in the church. I didn't even know what that meant. I remember telling my girlfriend on a phone call, "I'm a new man, I'm a Christian now, and I'm going to be a leader in the church." She said, "You mean like a pastor?" I shrugged and said, "Yeah, I guess."

I had no idea what a pastor was—I just knew God had spoken something deep into my spirit. I even had this vision: I'd start a church and call it *The Table*. Because that cold metal table in the jail pod—that's where I really met God for the first time.

The Holy Spirit started transforming me. One of the first things He addressed was my mouth—my language. I was still cussing, still talking ghetto street talk. But little by little, He helped me change that. It wasn't easy, I was a "Born Again" baby Christian in a county jail surrounded by drug dealers, murderers, rapists, and thieves. But somehow, I was changing.

I felt free even though I still wrestled with anger and a long list of other things. But I kept chasing after Jesus. At first, I chased religion too, and that confused me. But God used it all. Eventually, I got transferred to federal prison. That opened up even more spiritual exposure. In federal prison, you can practice any religion. I explored everything—Native American sweat lodges, Judaism, paganism. I was searching for the Truth.

One time, I sat in a Native American sweat lodge with some Southern Natives. They believed in Jesus, and I remember hearing them sing praises to the Lord in that dark, steamy place. It was beautiful. Even in the strangest places, Jesus kept showing up.

As I got to know Jesus more, I started to hear His voice more clearly. I was beginning to discern who God was, who the Holy Spirit was, and what the Truth really was. So, as I visited different religions—Mormonism, Catholicism, and others no matter which service I went to, I started to recognize the lies. The things that had been added to the Bible but weren't truly in God's Word. I could see the fingerprints of man-made religion all over it. I could sense that something was wrong.

Eventually, He made something clear to me: **"All I want from you is a relationship, not religion."** That moment changed everything. I didn't want religion—I wanted a real relationship with God. I wanted to be the best follower of Jesus I could be. A true Christian.

Right now, I want to ask you—do you want that same real relationship with God—the One who can bring you out of darkness and into the light? If your heart is longing for something more, if you're tired of the chaos, anxiety, depression, or the fake religions that surround you then this moment is for you.

The Bible says in Romans 10:9, "If you confess with your mouth, 'Jesus is Lord,' and believe in your heart that God raised Him from the dead, you will be saved." That's it. It's faith. Faith in Jesus. Faith in the power of His resurrection. He died on the cross for your sins, and He rose again so that He could be your Lord and best friend.

So, if that is your desire, right now confess with your mouth that Jesus is Lord, believe in your heart that God raised Him from the dead, because He did. He's alive. And this is your opportunity to believe in Him. You don't have to say it perfectly. Just be real. Pray in your own words. That's what I did, I put my faith in Jesus, and everything changed.

Now let me tell you something important. If you just did that—if you believed and confessed Jesus as Lord and that He was raised from the dead by God—you are a now a new creation. Born again. The Spirit of God now lives inside of you. Incredible, right?

But it's also serious. You've now stepped into a new life, and there is a real enemy, the devil—who will try to steal that truth from you. He hates everything God is doing in you. That's why you've got to press in. Get a Bible—maybe a New King James Version. Start reading it daily, just like I did. Talk to God. Spend time with Him. Build your relationship with Him like your life depends on it— because it does.

So, becoming a true Christian: I began to devour His Word even more. I dreamed of getting married one day, doing things the right way, being a good man—a faithful husband, an honorable citizen. I didn't want to steal or sell drugs ever again. I started listening to different music.

That old gangsta rap was losing its grip on me. It didn't speak to who I was anymore. God was doing something new. And still, I wrestled.

I didn't understand why I wasn't completely free yet. I didn't know enough to recognize spiritual strongholds. And yes, I messed up. I smoked spice in prison— a synthetic drug that's easy to get in there. I got high a few times. But the last time I did, I felt something shift again.

I went to my cell, and the door slammed shut behind me. It felt like I was never going to get out. I prayed: *"God, take this addiction from me. I surrender it."* That was it. The next day, I woke up and knew—I was done. My drug addiction was gone. That was my last time getting high.

Jesus had set me free.

GOD'S GRACE

Chapter 5

If you're a new believer, get ready—God's about to take you deeper. And if you've walked with Jesus for years, don't think you've seen it all. There's more— so much more. Something powerful in this book is waiting for you, and it's going to shake you—in the best, most life-changing way.

The rest of my time in prison seemed to go by pretty quickly. I stayed busy in the art room, prayer meetings, church services and Bible studies. Day by day, I kept surrendering different parts of my heart—my pride, my false identity and the tough guy act I had clung to for so long.

IT WAS NOT EASY!

If you've never been on the streets or in prison, it's *extremely* political and *deeply* racist. In the feds, you kind of "click up" with the hood you're from or who you look like.

You don't really get a choice. You either stay with your own race, gang or you run independent—and running independent comes with its own dangers.

Being the knucklehead I was when I first got there, I just stuck with the white dudes. I was a bald-headed white guy, so it made sense on the surface. The crazy part is before prison, I hung out with everyone— Mexican gangs, white supremacists, whoever. I just knew everyone.

But under the surface, I continued to surrender the tough guy act. Little by little, the Lord kept whispering, asking more of me. He was calling me to step away completely from the people I was still running with, no matter what it might cost. That kind of move in prison can get you hurt. But when I stepped out in faith, something unexpected happened. The respect I had built, and the change they saw in me, made a way. They let me go without a fight. That alone was a miracle.

God taught me so much during that season. I also connected with some real Christian brothers, some of whom I still talk with today. I wasn't just surviving anymore, I was *growing*. I still remember my final days there. The feeling that I would never again be locked up was overwhelming. I somehow knew the only time I would ever step foot inside a jail or prison again would be to *minister the Word of God*.

Saying goodbye was emotional. There was an older man I called my "pops"—he had become like a father figure to me. He was doing a life sentence. But by the grace of God—and after a lot of prayers—he's out today. God showed His mercy even in places where the world says there's no hope.

I remember the last day very clearly—God's favor was all over it. Most released inmates get a bus ticket back to wherever they came from, usually some long, uncomfortable ride from the prison to their old life. That's what I was expecting too—a grueling bus trip from Colorado to Utah. But God had other plans. His favor showed up in the details, and I was given a plane ticket instead.

So, there I was, standing in the airport: no shackles, no chains, just me, boarding a flight for the first time as a free man. I couldn't help but laugh a little. It felt surreal. I was walking through that airport like someone stepping onto a different planet. Everyone around me was buried in their phones, moving fast, distracted by everything. But not me. I was fully present. I was alive. I was on fire for the Lord, and I didn't want to lose what He had started in me.

When I landed in Utah and got to the halfway house, I didn't have much—just a few hundred bucks from my artwork, no car, no place of my own—but I had faith. Real faith. And I was determined to bless God back, to show Him just how thankful I was that He never gave up on me.

At that time, my sister was still in my life. She brought me some clothes and helped where she could. But outside of that, I didn't have any family who could support me. It was just me and God. New city, new life. New man. I had to relearn how to live. I had to unlearn the streets.

I had to ask God every single day—lead me, teach me, guide me—and He did. He kept breathing life into me every step of the way.

Eventually, God opened a door for me to get a job. The men who owned the company knew my background, but they gave me a chance anyway. They were supportive. They helped me get my first car and my first apartment outside of the halfway house. God used them to help establish me in this new season. If you're reading this and you're stepping out of that same dark place— listen to me, really listen. Rely on God. He will provide everything you need, step by step. It may not happen overnight, but if you stay faithful to Him, He will show up in ways you can't even imagine.

While I was still living at the halfway house, I started visiting different Christian churches. It was amazing. The worship moved me deeply, and I met so many wonderful people who loved the Lord and welcomed me just as I was.

I kept praying, "God, where do You want me? What church do I belong to?" I knew that the "Church" as a whole was the body of Christ, but I was starting to recognize that there were many different parts—and I wanted to be planted in the part of the body where I could thrive, where I could serve and grow and be the best son I could be to my Heavenly Father. And little by little, He kept guiding me.

My time in the halfway house was short, and I was stepping into the rest of my 30s as a new man—it felt wonderful. The drugs and chaos that floated through the halfway house never touched me. I was on fire for the Lord. I was focused, hungry for more of Him, and ready to hit the streets running.

I wanted to start dating—but honestly, it was scary. After being locked up for years, suddenly there were women everywhere. It was overwhelming. I wasn't used to that kind of freedom. But I kept praying, "God, You heard my prayers; You know my heart. I know You have the perfect Christian woman for me. I'm trusting You with this."

The journey had just begun, and God was just getting started. I truly wanted to live out His will. I wanted to do things the right way—His way, not mine. I wanted to be successful in all areas: spiritually, financially, relationally. No more fornication. No more using women. No more robbing or manipulating to get ahead. I was determined to do it right.

Then one day, something unexpected happened. A friend of mine, someone I'd known for a long time called his mom and told her, "You should invite Zack to that Christian concert," so she did. She reached out and asked if I wanted to go. I wasn't sure at first, but I had this excitement in my spirit.

I remembered a Christian movie I saw while I was locked up, where the main character met his wife at a concert. Deep down, I hoped maybe this would be that moment for me too. Come to find out my friend's sister and her two kids were with his mom. I had never met his sister before then; we had lived completely different lives.

But when I saw her, I thought, *Wow… she's cute.*

Watching her worship at that concert was amazing. I didn't know much about her yet, just that she had two kids, so I figured she was probably married, and that was that.

A short while later, I had posted some of my artwork on Facebook, and she reached out and asked if I would illustrate a children's book she had written in college. We started talking first through messages, then on the phone and after about a month, we finally decided to meet up. It was December 23rd, 2016, and it felt like God had written the whole thing like a Hallmark movie.

We went out to eat, then ice skated afterward. We hardly talked about the book. I wanted to kiss her, but I didn't. It was innocent and beautiful. We were both still immature, though. She had already been through two divorces and carried a lot of childhood trauma. I was still learning how to walk as a new man. But I wanted a woman in my life so badly.

We started dating and eventually fell into fornication. But even in the middle of our mess, we were growing in our love for God and each other. One year later, on December 23rd, I proposed at the same place where we had our first date. Six months later, we were married. Our honeymoon turned into a week-long drinking binge, and that pattern continued afterward. We kept drinking, arguing, and fighting—which led to us separating just four months after we were married.

It was one of the hardest seasons of my life. We spent seven months apart. Grueling, painful months. I was overwhelmed. I didn't know how to be a husband. I didn't know how to be a stepfather. I kept praying, asking God to teach me how to do all these things—but the truth was, I was still wrestling with trauma, with strongholds, with demons from my past that I hadn't fully faced.

During that time apart, I made some terrible choices. Even though I was still going to church every Sunday, I met another woman.

And in my twisted, broken thinking, I ended up sleeping with her. I was living in adultery. I was drinking and partying again. I never went back to drugs, but the drinking had me in a chokehold.

Then came the day everything changed.

It was the day before Mother's Day, the same day I lost my mom. Earlier that day, my wife and I had gotten into a huge fight over the phone. That night, I went to the club and got more drunk than I ever had in my life. I ended up stumbling down the street, and, for some reason, I called my wife.

She came and picked me up. What I didn't know was that earlier that same day, she had been praying for me—with her mom and a friend—refusing to give up on me. She wasn't about to let another marriage end in divorce.

And somehow… God moved.

God brought my wife back to me on the very same day I lost my mother. It was like He reached down into the middle of my chaos, my mess, and said, *"I'm not done with you yet."*

NEW BEGINNINGS
Chapter 6

I need you to know something before we go any further.

Years ago, while attending a conference at God's Place, the prophetic voice of **Prophet Bobby Conner**— a seasoned and authentic man of God—called me out and spoke a word that wrecked me. He said I was to write a book. Not just any book—a book about *how God can bring you out of the places that you put yourself into* (yes, that was the exact phrase).

To be honest, I was in disbelief. I wasn't even that familiar with the prophetic at the time. And me? A writer? I'm a horrible speller. I barely made it through English class without cheating and my mom's help. I struggled with reading most of my life. So why would God ask **me** to write a book—*about how God can bring you out of the places that you put yourself into*?

But that prophetic word didn't just confirm something—It ignited something. Deep inside, I already knew my story wasn't just mine. It was a weapon. A roadmap. A key that could unlock prison doors for others. Because it's one thing to get saved. It's another thing to get free.

That's why I'm telling you my story—the addiction, the crime, the trauma, the prison time, the heartbreak. Not to glorify any of it. Not for shock value. I'm telling it because I need you to see **your** story inside **mine**. Maybe you never touched meth. Maybe you've never been to jail. But I promise you this: you've faced something. Shame. Fear. Rejection. Cycles you couldn't break. Lies that wrapped around your identity and wouldn't let go. That's why this book exists.

Because whether the chains are visible or invisible, bondage is still bondage. And the devil doesn't usually show up shouting—he whispers. He plants thoughts. He twists truth. And little by little, we come into agreement with him.

We believe the lie that says, *"You'll never be free."* Or *"This is just who you are."*

Those lies led me into dark places. And maybe, in your own way, they've led you too. But here's the truth that will change everything: **Only God can bring you out.** Not just out of addiction or outward sin, but out of the deep inner places where those lies took root. The parts of your soul that shaped your identity, your reactions, and your relationships.

That's where the enemy works—and that's exactly where God wants to heal you. So, as you keep reading, don't just see my story. Ask the Holy Spirit to show you yours. Ask Him to reveal the lies you've believed, the doors that were opened, and the silent agreements you didn't even know you made. Because once the truth is revealed…

Freedom follows.

After God brought my wife and me back together, things started to move fast. It was beautiful, yes—but also messy. We had been through so much—trauma, near divorce, addiction, strongholds we didn't even have language for yet. Our love was real, but we were still learning how to fight the right battles. Early on, we had some arguments, nothing major, but enough to trigger old emotions in both of us. I still wrestled with drinking. One evening, we went out to eat, and I ordered a drink. But my wife stood her ground and said, "No." That moment flipped a switch in me.

I snapped.

I remember standing up in the middle of the restaurant, yelling. I stormed out and walked down the street, screaming at God. I must've looked completely crazy. But I know now—that wasn't just emotion. That was a spirit manifesting. It didn't want to let go. It had claimed a right to my life through alcohol. But I cried out to God for freedom. And that's exactly what I got.

My wife chased me down in the car, found me, and pulled me in. From that day on, alcohol has never been an issue for us. I was set free.

During our separation, my wife had already gone through layers of healing and deliverance—breaking off childhood trauma, rejection, fear, alcoholism, and more. She had been digging into the Word, fasting, praying, fighting for our marriage even when I didn't deserve it. Her obedience laid a foundation I didn't even understand at the time.

When we got back together, God began opening doors. I got off probation early—just in time to apply for a passport. Miraculously, I got it in less than a week. Even more miraculously, we had the money to go on a trip with our church... to Israel. Walking where Jesus walked standing in Jerusalem, floating on the Sea of Galilee and walking the same land the disciples had walked.

I'm telling you—it brought the Bible to life. Something changed in me. It felt like we were part of a much bigger story, and God was inviting us into it.

When we got back home, we jumped into ministry. I started a recovery group at the church. My wife joined the board. We were busy. We were living in a townhouse at that time, but April kept saying, "We need a house." Within a year, we were under contract to build a brand-new home. Miracle after miracle. God was establishing us—not just practically, but spiritually.

But we weren't satisfied just going to church. We hit the streets, malls and stores. We went treasure hunting—asking God to lead us to people who needed Him. Time and time again, He showed up: prophetic words, words of knowledge, healings and deliverance. The Holy Spirit was teaching us in real time, and everyone around us seemed to notice. People kept saying, "You're called." "You're anointed." "You should join our ministry!"

But even in the middle of all that fruit, God started to shift us again. My wife and I began to feel stirred. The Holy Spirit was leading us to leave the church we had been part of—the one where we had found a sense of belonging.

She stepped off the board. I handed off the recovery group. It wasn't out of frustration or division—it was obedience. God was calling us to a new place. A new assignment. And just like I had prayed back in the halfway house, asking God to lead me to the church where I belonged, He answered. A new place. A new tribe. A place where we could grow deeper and be sharpened. We were home. And that's when God began pressing into even deeper things.

I couldn't stop thinking, "Why do I still struggle? Why did I smoke spice in prison, even after I got saved? Why did I manipulate, lie, and fall into drinking again after being free for so long?"

I needed to know.

I didn't want to keep walking around with unanswered questions. I didn't want to stay bound, so I started to study. I asked God to take me deeper. And He did.

He led me to study the heart—not just emotionally, but biblically. I started tracing things back to the beginning: Genesis, Adam, the fall, the curse, the promises. I started learning about the difference between spirit, soul, and body—and how many of the things we call "sin" are actually rooted in soul wounds or demonic strongholds that have never been dealt with. Suddenly, everything started making sense: the drug addiction, the broken relationships, the outbursts of rage, the shame.

It wasn't just bad behavior. It was bad beliefs. Deep-rooted lies in my soul—some planted by trauma, some by my own sin, and others directly by the enemy. Lies that shaped my identity, my reactions, my relationships, even how I viewed God.

I thought being saved would fix everything. But what I didn't realize is that my spirit was saved—but my soul was still wounded. My soul still believed the old stories. And those stories needed to be replaced with truth. That's when God began the process of real deliverance.

So, if you've made it this far—don't stop. We're about to go into the parts most people skip. The parts that turn saved believers into free believers. The parts that took me from simply surviving… to walking in authority, to living in peace, to being used by God to set others free. You're not reading this by accident. God brought you here.

And now it's time to go deeper.

SPIRIT, SOUL AND BODY

Chapter 7

Before we go any deeper, I need to make something very clear. Not everyone ends up in darkness because of their choices. Yes, this book is about how God brings us out of the places we put ourselves into—but that's not the whole picture. Many people were dragged into dark places by things they didn't choose. People have been mentally and physically abused, abandoned, molested, lied to, and even trafficked. Kids have been exposed to porn, violence, and addiction before they ever had a chance to know who they were. That wasn't their sin; that was the enemy's strategy.

I didn't choose to find those magazines in my mom's closet while playing hide-and-seek. I didn't ask to be shaped by addiction, or abandonment, or the violence I grew up around. That's how the devil works. He starts young. He builds strongholds early. He uses lies as bait, then locks people in with a choice.

Some of us opened the doors. Some had them kicked open. But either way, Jesus is still the only One who can bring you out.

Okay—let's go deeper.

"Now may the God of peace Himself sanctify you completely; and may your whole spirit, soul, and body be preserved blameless at the coming of our Lord Jesus Christ." —1 Thessalonians 5:23 (NKJV)

This verse changed everything for me. It explained what I had been wrestling with since the moment I got saved. I knew something happened. It wasn't emotional hype—it was real. I felt peace I had never known. Something inside me came alive. But I was still a mess. Even though I was reading my Bible, going to services, and praying, I started asking, "Am I really saved?" That's when God started showing me how I was made—and how He planned to heal me.

You are made of three parts: spirit, soul, and body. Your spirit is the part of you that was dead and comes alive when you're born again. It's where the Holy Spirit dwells. Your soul is your mind, will, and emotions. It's where trauma lives. It's where memories live. It's where strongholds are built. Your body is the flesh. Your physical shell. The part trained by sin, habits, and cravings. Paul didn't say, "God will sanctify your spirit and forget the rest." He said completely— spirit, soul, and body. That means salvation is just the start. Wholeness is the goal.

When I started to go deeper, I began to realize why I could be saved and still not free. I had seen it in others and lived it myself. People get radically saved—crying, praying, hungry for God—and yet remain trapped in addiction, depression, lust, or rage. That was me. Even after being born again, I still needed deliverance. I didn't know demons could hide in my soul—in those dark places I tried to forget existed.

I had never heard a teaching on spirit, soul, and body. No one had explained why my faith was real, but my freedom wasn't complete. And it didn't make sense until I saw this truth: salvation heals your spirit, deliverance heals your soul, discipline trains your body. Jesus made my spirit new. But my soul still needed healing. My body still craved sin. My mind still thought like a hustler.

That's why I still talked like I was in the streets, why I smoked spice even after reading the Word, why I flipped out at my wife at a restaurant just because she told me I shouldn't drink. That wasn't just my flesh. That wasn't just a "struggle." That was bondage in my soul. That was a demon fighting for territory. Some of you have tried everything. You've prayed, fasted, and cried. And you're wondering, "Why am I still stuck?" Because you might be trying to counsel a demon or cast out a soul wound—and it doesn't work that way.

Demons need to be cast out. Wounds need to be healed. Lies need to be replaced. Habits need to be retrained.

That's why I couldn't get free from porn until I broke agreement with the lie that I'd always be perverted. That's why I couldn't break addiction until I repented, renounced, and got delivered. That's why rage didn't leave until I let the Holy Spirit walk into that place of trauma—the one where I learned violence was the only way to be heard.

Jesus didn't die just to give you a better afterlife. He died to make you whole right now. He took your pain. He broke your curse. He gave you access to the Father. He made your spirit alive. He sent His Spirit to walk you into freedom—every part of you. That means if you still feel tormented, it doesn't mean you're not saved. But it does mean God has more for you. You don't have to stay in survival mode. You don't have to carry shame or cycles or cravings. The same Jesus who met me in that cold jail pod wants to meet you—spirit, soul, and body.

Reflection Questions:

Have you been focusing only on your spirit while neglecting your soul or body?

Are there wounds, memories, or patterns of behavior that still shape the way you think, feel, or respond to life?

Take a moment to consider—what part of your temple have you not yet allowed Jesus to enter and restore?

Prayer:

Father God, thank You for saving my spirit. But I know You want all of me. So, I open the doors to my soul for You. Heal what's broken. Shine Your light into every place. Show me what I've believed that's not from You. Deliver me from every lie, every spirit, and every trauma that's still gripping me. And teach my body to follow. I want to be made whole—spirit, soul, and body. In Your name, Jesus. Amen.

NOTES

CAN A CHRISTIAN HAVE A DEMON?

Chapter 8

"My people are destroyed for lack of knowledge…"

Hosea 4:6 (NKJV)

This question is one of the most controversial in the Church today, but it's also one of the most important: Can a Christian have a demon? I've seen the answer up close. I've seen people worship on Sunday and battle torment on Monday. I've seen leaders fall into hidden sin, believers wrestle with suicidal thoughts, and youth on fire for God still held captive by demonic oppression.

But I've also seen those same people—including myself—get free. So, here's my answer, and it's not just based on experience, but backed by Scripture: Yes, a Christian can have a demon—but a demon cannot have a Christian.

The confusion usually comes from not understanding the difference between possession and oppression. Possession means total ownership and control. That's not possible for a born-again believer. Your spirit is sealed with the Holy Spirit (Ephesians 1:13). Oppression, however, means to be influenced, tormented, or bound in part of your being—especially your soul or body. When someone gets saved, their spirit is made new, but their soul may still carry the effects of trauma, sin, and lies. If those areas haven't been surrendered and healed, demons can still take up residence there—**NOT IN YOUR SPIRIT**, but in your soul, or flesh.

I was saved in prison. No one had to convince me demons were real, I knew it. What I didn't know was that they were still affecting me after I gave my life to Christ. I thought getting saved meant everything would automatically get better. But I was still battling violent anger, deep depression, perverted thoughts, and suicidal urges. I was born again… but I was also bound.

Ephesians 4:27 says, "Nor give place to the devil." That means it's possible to give the enemy a place, even as a believer. That place could be a trauma never healed, a sin never confessed, a lie never replaced with truth, or a habit that opened a door to darkness.

Demons don't need permission to knock, but they need a legal right to stay. And when we agree with lies, entertain sin, or live in unrepented areas, it gives them a foothold. It doesn't mean you're not saved. It means part of your soul still needs the freedom Jesus died to give you. Some argue, "There's no verse that says a Christian had a demon." That's true. But there also isn't a verse that says a Christian can't.

What we do see are examples where believers clearly struggled with demonic influence: Jesus cast demons out of people in synagogues (Mark 1:21–27)—these were religious, practicing Jews. In Acts 5, Ananias and Sapphira were part of the early Church, but Satan "filled" their hearts to lie.

Paul warns believers to cast down arguments and take thoughts captive—because strongholds can exist in the mind after salvation (2 Corinthians 10:4–5).

I've personally ministered deliverance to believers filled with the Holy Spirit and speaking in tongues yet still tormented by demonic influence. When we prayed, the demons manifested, screamed, and left. The person felt peace for the first time in years. That's real freedom.

Maybe that's you. Maybe you're reading this and thinking, "I love God, but I'm still in a fight. I still feel tormented, tempted, or trapped."

You're not crazy.

You're not weak.

You're in a war.

And this war isn't just mental or emotional, it's spiritual. The enemy doesn't care that you go to church. He cares when you get free.

He'll do whatever he can to stay hidden—because demons love darkness. And religion has helped them hide.

But Jesus came to set the captives free—not just the lost, but also His followers. And He's still doing it today. This isn't a debate between salvation or deliverance. It's both. Jesus saves your spirit and delivers your soul. He forgives you and heals you. He gives you peace and drives out torment.

Reflection Questions:

Have you ever assumed your struggles were "just flesh" and not considered a spiritual influence?

What patterns in your life seem too strong to break without help?

Are you willing to let the Holy Spirit shine a light in every part of your life—even if it gets uncomfortable?

Prayer:

Jesus, thank You for saving me. I believe Your blood is enough, but I also know I need Your power to deliver me from anything still holding me back. I open my heart to You—spirit, soul, and body. Show me if there's any area where the enemy has access. I want to be completely free. In Your name, Jesus. Amen.

NOTES

THE PLACES WITHIN

Chapter 9

"Do you not know that you are the temple of God and that the Spirit of God dwells in you?"

1 Corinthians 3:16 (NKJV)

I didn't realize it at first, but I was a temple with many places I hadn't given to God. Some of those places were full of pain. Others were sealed up with secrets. Some were buried under years of trauma and lies—areas of my soul that I hadn't even considered letting Jesus into. But He wanted all of me.

Deliverance doesn't just happen during a service or with someone shouting on a stage. Sometimes it happens in the quiet places—when the Holy Spirit walks through the corridors of your soul and begins to knock on doors you thought were sealed shut. And when He does, what's been hiding must come into the light.

At first, I just knew there were broken places in me. I didn't have words for it—I just felt it: the depression, the anger, the torment.

I didn't know why I still felt so heavy when I was reading my Bible and praying. Then I came across a book that changed everything— *The Secrets to Deliverance* by **Apostle Alexander Pagani**. In that book, he explained in detail that Christians are called temples by Jesus, and how temples have many rooms, and how demons could be hiding in those dark rooms they haven't surrendered. That word hit me like a bolt of lightning. Suddenly it all started to click.

I realized God had been trying to show me the same thing: there were rooms inside me I had never opened. Some I had sealed off because of pain. Others I didn't even know existed. But Jesus knew. And He wasn't trying to shame me—He was trying to free me.

It made me think about the temple in the Old Testament. It had the outer courts, the inner courts, and the Most Holy Place. Just like that temple, we are made up of three parts—spirit, soul, and body. When you're born again, God comes to dwell in your spirit—the most inner place. But the soul and the body? Those places still need to be sanctified. And if you don't let Jesus into those areas, the enemy will try to stay there.

I had places of rage—rooms where violence had become my survival. I had places of lust—where early exposure to porn and perversion had twisted my view of love. I had places of shame—where the voice of the enemy whispered, "You'll never be clean." I had given Jesus the living room, but those hidden rooms, I kept them locked, thinking He didn't need to go there. But He already knew what was in them.

When I finally surrendered those areas to the Lord, everything began to change. Demons that had been hiding for years started to surface. Not because I was possessed.

But because I had pain they were attached to—and that pain had never been healed. See, demons don't just live off sin—they live off wounds, lies, and darkness. They hide in the places that haven't been exposed to the Light: places of trauma, bitterness, unforgiveness, generational patterns. And if those places never get healed, the enemy stays hidden—undetected but still active. That's why some believers stay stuck in the same cycles for years.

It's not because they don't love God. It's because something in the house hasn't been dealt with. But there's good news. You don't have to live that way. The moment you say yes to Jesus—fully yes—He steps into every place with power.

When I finally said, "God, You can have it all," things started breaking off me. I wept. I shook. I confessed. I repented. And I healed. Not all in one night—but one place at a time. Remember this: the Holy Spirit does not stop knocking. Because He loves you too much to leave you partially free.

Reflection Questions:

What areas of your life have you kept closed off from God?

What past wounds or lies might still be influencing how you think or react?

Are you willing to invite the Holy Spirit into every place of your soul?

Prayer:

Holy Spirit, I give You full access. Every memory, every pain, every hidden place. I don't want to keep anything locked away from You. I trust You to shine Your light and drive out anything that's been hiding in the dark. I surrender it all to You. In Your name, Jesus. Amen.

NOTES

BATTLEFIELD IN THE MIND

Chapter 10

"For the weapons of our warfare are not carnal but mighty in God for pulling down strongholds, casting down arguments and every high thing that exalts itself against the knowledge of God, bringing every thought into captivity to the obedience of Christ." —2 Corinthians 10:4–5 (NKJV)

Deliverance is not just about casting out demons—it's about renewing the mind. Because what good is it to cast something out if the lie that let it in is still there? Let me say it this way: demons are often the symptoms but lies are the root. Even after I had been saved and delivered from drug addiction and drinking, I still struggled. I knew God. I prayed. I worshiped. But there were thoughts in my head that didn't match the Word. And I didn't recognize that those thoughts were building something inside me—a structure, a prison, a stronghold.

The mind is a battlefield, and every thought we agree with either partners with God or with the enemy. Every thought becomes a building block—either for the Kingdom of Truth or the kingdom of lies. And the enemy is subtle. He doesn't always scream. Sometimes he whispers, and sometimes that whisper sounds like your own voice. Paul called them "strongholds" for a reason. These aren't surface-level thoughts.

They're deeply held beliefs that shape your identity, your emotions, and your decisions. For years, I believed things that felt true but weren't: "I'll always be angry. That's just who I am." "I'm broken because of what happened to me. I'll never be whole." "God can forgive others, but not me." "I'm too messed up to be used by God." Those weren't just negative thoughts. They were lies. Lies that had gained access, grown roots, and built walls. And the more I agreed with them, the more power they had. The enemy doesn't need your permission to lie. But he does need your agreement to build a stronghold. And if he can convince you to agree with a lie, he can influence how you live.

Deliverance confronts the demonic, but freedom is sustained by truth. That means you can cast a spirit out, but if the blueprint in your mind isn't changed, that spirit might come back—and bring seven more with it. You can't cast out a lie. You must replace it with the Truth. Romans 12:2 says, "Do not be conformed to this world, but be transformed by the renewing of your mind." That's not a one-time event. It's a process. It's daily. It's intentional.

For me, that meant learning to speak truth out loud. When I felt worthless, I declared, "I am chosen, holy, and blameless in His sight" (Ephesians 1:4). When I felt tempted and weak, I declared, "Sin shall not have dominion over me" (Romans 6:14). When depression whispered death, I declared, "I shall not die, but live, and declare the works of the Lord" (Psalm 118:17) That's how you fight. With the Word of God, with Truth. And yes—it's a fight.

But it's a fight YOU CAN WIN.

Reflection Questions:

What thoughts have you believed that don't line up with God's Word?

Can you trace those thoughts back to trauma, pain, or past experiences?

Are you ready to break agreement with those lies and replace them with truth?

Prayer:

Father, I repent for believing lies about You, about myself, and about my future. I renounce every agreement I've made with the enemy. I tear down every stronghold in my mind and declare Your truth over my life. Let my mind be renewed by Your Word, and let every lie be silenced by Your voice. In Your name, Jesus. Amen.

NOTES

THE DOORS WE LEAVE OPEN

Chapter 11

"Nor give place to the devil." —Ephesians 4:27 (NKJV)

Freedom isn't just about getting free. It's about staying free. That's where many people miss it. They think deliverance is a one-time event, but it's a lifestyle. And one of the biggest reasons Christians stay bound is because they don't realize they've left spiritual doors open—and the enemy walked right in.

I saw this firsthand. After getting saved in jail and experiencing the presence of God, I was still tormented in my soul. Even though I had prayed, repented, and given my life to Jesus, parts of me still felt like a war zone. I would feel free for a while, then the depression would return, the sexual immorality, the rage and the shame. It wasn't until I started to go deeper—asking the Holy Spirit to show me the places I had never surrendered—that I began to understand.

Some of those places in my soul had been shaped by trauma. Others had been opened by sin. And some were just wide-open doors because of my ignorance.

I had watched porn since childhood. I had smoked meth for years. I had practiced manipulation, lust, and rage like it was second nature. I had been abused and abandoned. I didn't know that all those things left open doors. Demons need legal permission to stay. Even in unbelievers, they look for legal ground. How much more in a believer? Your spirit is sealed by the Holy Spirit. But your soul and body are still being sanctified. And if you don't guard them, you'll find yourself bound again, wondering what happened.

The Bible says, "Nor give place to the devil" (Ephesians 4:27). That word "place" in the Greek is *topos*. It means a specific territory, a space, a room, or a legal ground. When I read that, everything clicked. I realized I had given the enemy topos—places in my soul he had no right to, but I had never taken them back.

Back in Chapter One, I talked about growing up with no boundaries, no real guidance. The lifestyle my mom lived was wide open to the enemy. Not because she was evil, but because she was broken. So was her mom. That generational pain and compromise created doorways. And I walked right through them. So, let's talk about the most common doorways I've seen—in my own life and in the lives of those I've ministered to:

Unforgiveness. Jesus was clear in Matthew 18: if we don't forgive, we hand ourselves over to torment. I had to forgive people who mistreated me, used me, rejected me, left me. It wasn't easy. But as long as I held bitterness, the door stayed open.

Sexual Sin. **Pornography**. **Fornication**. Soul ties. I carried perversion deep into my Christian walk. Every time I gave into it, the doorway opened again. The Bible says, "Flee sexual immorality. Every sin that a man does is outside the body, but he who commits sexual immorality sins against his own body" (1 Corinthians 6:18, NKJV).

Substance Abuse. The Bible calls witchcraft *pharmakeia*. That's where we get our word for pharmacy. Drugs and alcohol don't just affect your body—they open your soul. I smoked meth and other drugs for years. I even drank after salvation. Each time I did, I opened a door.

Occult Involvement. It sounds extreme, but things like horoscopes, sage, crystals, energy healing, yoga, ancestral rituals—all of it gives access to demonic influence. I had practiced witchcraft without knowing it , even though I had been around witches. It's real, and it opens real doors.

Trauma. This one is often overlooked. Not every door is opened by sin. Some are opened by pain. The night I found those magazines in my mom's closet—that was a trauma door. When I was rejected, abused, or abandoned—those were trauma doors. The enemy came in and whispered lies: "You're dirty. You're unlovable. You'll always be this way." Even if you didn't open the door, the wound is real. And it must be healed.

So how do you shut the doors? It doesn't start with trying harder. It starts with surrender. I had to go through a process: I asked the Holy Spirit to reveal every open door. I repented of sin and unforgiveness. I renounced agreements with darkness. I cast out every spirit that had come through those doors. I asked the Holy Spirit to fill every place. And then—I started guarding those doors with truth and obedience.

Jesus gave a warning in Matthew 12. He said when a demon leaves, it goes looking for rest. If it finds none, it comes back to the house it left. If it finds that house "empty, swept, and put in order," it brings seven more demons, and the person ends up worse than before. The key word there is empty.

You can't just clean house. You have to fill it.

That means with Jesus, the Word of God, prayer, worship, community, discipline and intimacy with the Holy Spirit. It means getting honest, breaking habits, setting boundaries and asking for help.

Freedom without discipline is like a door with no lock. And I was tired of getting robbed.

The truth is, God had already delivered me. But I had to learn how to walk in that deliverance. I had to stop calling sin a "struggle." I had to let the Holy Spirit convict me instead of making excuses. I had to stop blaming everyone else and start shutting the doors.

Reflection Questions:

What areas of your life might be open doors to the enemy?

Is there anything you've been calling a "struggle" that may actually be a spiritual foothold?

Are you ready to fully surrender and shut every door to the enemy?

Prayer:

Jesus, I ask You to search me and show me any door I've left open. I repent for every sin, every agreement, and every habit that gave the enemy a place. I renounce every unclean spirit and break every tie to darkness. I command every spirit to leave in Your name. Fill every part of me with Your Holy Spirit. Teach me to guard my heart and walk in Truth. In Your name, Jesus. Amen.

NOTES

WHAT DOES IT LOOK LIKE?

Chapter 12

"When evening had come, they brought to Him many who were demon-possessed. And He cast out the spirits with a word, and healed all who were sick." —Matthew 8:16 (NKJV).

Deliverance is real. It's not just emotional healing or a quiet inner shift. When the power of God confronts the presence of demons, things happen. And while deliverance is rooted in the authority of Jesus—not in feelings or reactions—there are times when the soul and body respond in undeniable ways.

I've seen people scream, shake, cough, vomit, fall to the floor, or suddenly remember trauma that had been buried for decades. I've felt the atmosphere shift when a spirit was exposed. And looking back now, I can see it in my own life too.

At the time, I didn't know what was happening. But now I understand that what I thought were just emotional outbursts were actually moments of deliverance. Like the time I stood up in the middle of a restaurant and stormed out, yelling at my wife and screaming at God. I now believe that it was a demon manifesting and being forced to leave. I didn't know it then—but I was being delivered.

All those moments of weeping, yelling, or shaking throughout my Christian walk—they weren't just emotional reactions. They were spiritual encounters. God was setting me free long before I had the language for it. That's the reality of manifestation. Let's be clear manifestation is not the goal.

FREEDOM IS!

Just because someone cries or coughs doesn't mean a demon left. And just because someone doesn't react outwardly doesn't mean they didn't get free. But the Bible does show us that demons often respond physically when confronted by the authority of Jesus:

In Mark 1:26, a demon cried out with a loud voice and came out.

In Mark 9:26, the spirit shrieked, convulsed violently, and came out.

In Luke 4:35, the demon threw the man down in their midst and came out without hurting him.

So yes, physical manifestations happen. But they're not the proof of deliverance— freedom afterward is. Don't fear the manifestation. Some people avoid deliverance because they're afraid of what might happen. Deliverance may feel uncomfortable—it is not unsafe when led by the Holy Spirit. You are not crazy. You are not possessed. You are being freed.

Think about it: if you've been carrying something in your soul or body for years—rage, trauma, fear, perversion—and it finally gets confronted, wouldn't your body respond? The physical reaction is often the soul and body releasing what was buried. It may look messy.

But so did the cross. And Jesus endured that mess so you could walk in freedom. Manifestations might look different for everyone, but here are common ways demons may react during deliverance: shaking or trembling, crying or screaming, yawning or coughing, nausea or vomiting, tightness in chest or head, sudden emotional outbursts, facial contortions or voices changing, remembering past trauma suddenly, feeling something leave or lift off you. Again— don't chase manifestations. But don't ignore them either. Let the Holy Spirit lead.

What I've seen as I've ministered to others, especially inmates, youth, and broken believers: A young man who had been trapped in sexual immorality broke down in sobs, screamed as the spirit of shame left, then collapsed in peace. A woman tormented by unforgiveness for years began to cough violently, then smile with peace for the first time in years. A brother in Christ, wrapped up in witchcraft, suddenly coughed and puked, and then sat up saying, "It's gone. I feel free."

The point isn't the drama. It's the deliverance. And every time I see it, I'm reminded Jesus is still setting captives free. After the Encounter, what comes next? Manifestation is not the finish line, it's the beginning. After someone gets delivered, here's what matters: fill the house with God–stay in prayer, worship, and the Word. Keep the doors closed– change what needs to change.

Renew the mind–keep speaking and living the truth. Get accountability–freedom grows in community. The enemy may try to come back. But when you're filled with the Spirit, grounded in truth, and walking in obedience—he has no place, no room, no house, no temple to come back to.

Reflection Questions:

Have you ever had an experience where your body or emotions responded to spiritual warfare?

Do manifestations scare you, or are you open to whatever God wants to do?

If you've been delivered, what have you done to fill the house and guard your freedom?

Prayer:

Holy Spirit, I give You permission to do whatever needs to be done in my life. I'm not afraid of how it looks—I want to be free. I trust You to lead me, protect me, and finish the work You've started. I surrender every reaction, every fear, every part of me to You. Let nothing remain hidden. In Your name, Jesus. Amen.

NOTES

FREEDOM IS A CHOICE

Chapter 13

"Stand fast therefore in the liberty by which Christ has made us free, and do not be entangled again with a yoke of bondage." —Galatians 5:1 (NKJV).

Getting free is one thing. Staying free is another. Deliverance is not a one-time prayer, it's a lifestyle. Freedom is something you walk out daily. You and I must keep moving forward after our chains hit the floor.

This is where many people miss it. They experience a powerful deliverance moment—demons flee, strongholds break, peace floods in. But then… life hits. Temptation returns. The thoughts come back. The flesh gets loud again. And they wonder, "Did I lose my freedom?" No. But now it's time to guard it. And that's a choice. A daily one. Freedom is God's gift—but walking in it is your decision.

When Lazarus was raised from the dead, Jesus said, "Loose him, and let him go." Resurrection brought him out of the grave. But someone still had to unwrap the grave clothes. That's what discipleship does. It teaches you how to think differently, live differently, respond differently. It helps you move from freedom in a moment to freedom as a way of life.

You don't need just a deliverance service—you need a daily surrender. And daily surrender is your responsibility. Jesus won't force it on you. It's up to you to choose to walk with Him. Paul said, "I discipline my body and bring it into subjection…" (1 Corinthians 9:27 NKJV). Why? Because freedom doesn't mean your flesh is silent, it means your spirit is in charge. It means you've chosen to live by the Spirit, not by your cravings.

God's Word renews your mind and keeps you grounded in truth. Lies lose power when truth becomes your default. "Your word I have hidden in my heart, that I might not sin against You." (Psalm 119:11 NKJV).

You must also guard your eyes and ears. What you feed grows. What you tolerate will eventually dominate. Music, shows, conversations, if they glorify sin, they're inviting the enemy back in. You choose what you let in.

Stay in prayer and worship. Prayer keeps your spirit tuned to God's voice. Worship shifts the atmosphere. You can't live in freedom and stay disconnected from the One who set you free. Walk in community. Isolation is a setup for relapse. You need people who challenge you, correct you, pray for you, and walk with you. And stay humble and watchful. Freedom isn't a badge—it's a gift.

Pride says, "I've got this now." But humility says, "God, I still need You every day." "Let him who thinks he stands take heed lest he fall." (1 Corinthians 10:12 NKJV) After deliverance, the enemy may try to come back. Not because you weren't set free—but because he's a squatter who hopes you won't guard your house. When the thoughts return, you take them captive.

When the temptations rise, you walk in the Spirit. When the enemy knocks, you don't answer—you declare the truth. This doesn't mean you live paranoid. It means you live prepared. And again—it's your choice to do so.

Jesus said, "Watch and pray, lest you enter into temptation…" (Mark 14:38 NKJV). You get to decide whether you'll stay watchful—or slide back. Ephesians 4:22–24 gives us the pattern: "Put off your old self… be renewed in the spirit of your mind… put on the new self…" You don't just cast out lust—you pursue purity. You don't just rebuke anger—you walk in peace. You don't just remove darkness—you fill yourself with light.

Every step forward in freedom comes down to a decision of your will.

NOBODY ELSE CAN DO IT FOR YOU.

Here's the best part—when you stay free, you help others get free.

Your testimony becomes a road map. Your breakthrough becomes someone else's hope. The same demons that tried to destroy you tremble when you walk into the room. This is what happened to me. I choose to stay free.

Reflection Questions:

What disciplines have you built to protect your freedom?

Are there areas in your life where old patterns are trying to return?

What choices do you need to make today to stay free?

Prayer:

Lord, thank You for the freedom You've given me. Help me to walk it out daily—with discipline, awareness, and boldness. I choose You today. I choose truth over lies, obedience over compromise, and surrender over pride. Show me where I need to guard my heart. Teach me how to feed my spirit, soul and body with You. Let my life reflect Your victory and let my freedom become a weapon that sets others free. In Your name, Jesus. Amen.

NOTES

HEALING THE SOUL

Chapter 14

"He heals the brokenhearted and binds up their wounds."
—Psalm 147:3 (NKJV)

Deliverance casts demons out, choosing freedom keeps the door shut, but inner healing binds the wounds they used to live in. I learned that the hard way. I thought if I could just get the demons out, and keep the door shut I'd be done. And yes, sometimes deliverance brings instant transformation. But for many of us, there's still a wounded soul underneath that needs the touch of Jesus. The souls needs to be saved.

James 1:21 (NKJV) says, "Therefore lay aside all filthiness and overflow of wickedness, and receive with meekness the implanted word, which is able to save your souls." He's writing that to believers. Our spirit is made alive when we get saved, but our soul—our mind, will, and emotions—is still being renewed, restored, and healed.

That's why I could be born again in prison and still carry the rejection from my father, the shame of what I'd done in the streets, and the fear that I'd never be enough for my wife. Those weren't demons anymore. But they were wounds that needed to be healed. I didn't understand that my soul was like a battlefield. Even after demons had been cast out, the cracks from trauma were still there.

Trauma is a door the enemy loves. But even after the spirits are evicted, trauma can remain in the soul like a shattered window. Imagine your soul like a mirror. Every time you're hurt, abused, rejected, or betrayed, it cracks a little more. And even after the demons leave, those cracks are still there until Jesus begins to heal them. That's why some people go through deliverance but still feel fragile. Still insecure. Still triggered. Still broken. Deliverance is the bulldozer. Healing is the reconstruction.

When Jesus stood up in the synagogue in Luke 4:18, He said, "The Spirit of the Lord is upon Me, because He has anointed Me to preach the gospel to the poor; He has sent Me to heal the brokenhearted, to proclaim liberty to the captives." He didn't just come to proclaim liberty. He came to heal the brokenhearted. Two assignments. One Savior. And both are for you.

When Jesus heals the soul, He goes deep. Not just into demonic oppression, but into all conditions. That's what happened to me in stages. He didn't do it all in one day, but He kept knocking on the places I tried to keep hidden: the ones formed when I found those magazines as a kid, the ones created when I heard my mom's voice for the last time and still didn't go see her, the ones formed in every toxic relationship and every lie I believed about who I was.

So how does He heal the soul?

He invites you into truth. He speaks into the pain. He walks you back to the moment it began and shows you where He was.

Forgiveness is another key. It's not about saying it was okay. It's about saying, "You don't owe me anymore." Jesus said if we don't forgive, we stay under torment. I had to forgive people who never apologized, who abused me, who hurt my family, who betrayed my trust. That forgiveness opened doors of healing I never thought were possible.

Then there were the soul ties: deep, unhealthy emotional and spiritual connections—formed through sex, trauma, and toxic bonds. I had to renounce them, one by one. Sometimes it was emotional. Sometimes I cried. But every time, I felt the Lord cutting away what had no place in my life anymore.

And last, but most important: Truth. Once the lie is exposed, it must be replaced with the truth. The lie said, "You're worthless." The truth says, "You are fearfully and wonderfully made." The lie said, "You'll always be broken." The truth says, "He who began a good work in you will complete it." The lie said, "You're too damaged to be used."

The truth says, "God chooses the foolish things to shame the wise." Healing doesn't mean you forget. It means the memory no longer crushes you. It doesn't mean the name never comes to mind, it means when it does, rage doesn't follow. It means the thought of your past brings gratitude, not guilt. That's the power of the blood of Jesus. That's what healing looks like.

I've watched inmates tear up with joy after forgiving their fathers. I've seen gang members sob like children as Jesus touched the places they never thought could be healed. I've held men who screamed in pain, then laughed in freedom as their soul was healed. That's what He came to do. Not just to cast demons out, but to make you whole.

Reflection Questions:

What pain have you buried that God might be asking to heal?

Have you gone through deliverance but still feel wounded inside?

Are you willing to let Jesus into those places—even if it's uncomfortable?

Prayer:

Jesus, I invite You into the places I've been hiding; into the memories, the pain, the wounds. I don't want to live patched up. I want to be made whole. I forgive those who hurt me. I break every soul tie. I renounce every lie. Heal my soul, Lord. Restore me from the inside out. In Your name, Jesus. Amen.

NOTES

AUTHORITY AND THE CROSS

Chapter 15

"Behold, I give you the authority to trample serpents and scorpions, and over all the power of the enemy, and nothing shall by any means hurt you." —Luke 10:19 (NKJV)

I used to think authority was something reserved for pastors, preachers, and the super-spiritual. I figured I'd never be qualified—I was just some ex-con who got radically saved in prison. But as I kept growing, as God kept teaching me, I realized something: the enemy's greatest fear isn't just Jesus—it's a believer who knows what Jesus gave them. And Jesus gave me something I never knew I had before: authority.

For so many years, I walked around thinking I had to beg God for freedom, beg Him to remove the demonic influence, beg Him to help me feel strong again.

I didn't know that He had already given me the authority to stand up and cast those demons out myself. I was praying like a victim, but God was calling me to pray like a victor. I didn't understand that when Jesus said, "It is finished," He didn't just mean the payment for sin—He meant the defeat of every stronghold, every curse, every demonic assignment over my life.

I remember back when I was still new in the faith, still on fire but also still untrained. I would be hit with thoughts—rage, perversion, depression—and I'd cry out to God, "Why is this still happening?" But I didn't realize those were enemies trying to reclaim lost territory. And they were banking on one thing:

That I wouldn't know the authority I had to stop them.

The devil is a legalist. He operates through access and agreement. But once I realized what the blood of Jesus did—how it stripped Satan of his rights over me—I started fighting differently. I wasn't just surviving anymore. I was pushing back.

The cross wasn't just an act of love. It was a declaration of war. Colossians 2:15 says that Jesus "disarmed principalities and powers, He made a public spectacle of them, triumphing over them in it." The cross stripped Satan of power. And when I got saved—really saved—Jesus handed me the keys. The same way I used to break into houses and steal things in my old life, now I was breaking into enemy territory and taking back what the devil stole from me: my peace, my mind, my identity. And here's the thing—this authority isn't just for me. It's for every believer. Luke 10:19 wasn't spoken to a church staff. It was spoken to everyday followers. Jesus said, "Behold, I give you authority…" Not because of who we are, but because of who He is.

I think back to all the times I got high, got arrested, or lost control—times I thought I was just broken or weak. But now I know I was under spiritual attack, and I didn't know how to fight. That's why this is so important. The cross didn't just save you—it empowered you.

The blood of Jesus cleansed your past, broke the curse, and gave you the legal right to trample every lie the devil ever used against you.

One time, I was ministering to someone who kept saying, "I feel like I'm not good enough to be free." And I stopped him and said, "Bro, it's not about being good enough—it's about the relationship Jesus paid for." That's the key. It's not our performance. It's our position. Ephesians 2:6 says we are "raised up together, and made to sit together in the heavenly places in Christ Jesus." That's not just a future promise. That's our current position. Authority comes from submission. James 4:7 says, "Therefore submit to God. Resist the devil and he will flee from you." Notice the order. Submission to God always comes before resistance of the enemy.

That means if you're walking in rebellion or compromise, you're handing your authority over. But the moment you submit—really surrender—your voice carries weight in the spirit.

I've cast out demons on the streets with no pastor around. I've seen inmates get set free by the name of Jesus alone. I've felt the power of darkness break under the authority of someone who simply believed the Word of God and stood on it. And I need you to know—you can do the same. You don't have to wait for a deliverance service. You don't need a pulpit. If you've surrendered your life to Christ, if you're filled with the Spirit, then you already have what you need. You've got the blood. You've got the Word. You've got the Name.

The cross wasn't just a rescue—it was a handoff. Jesus defeated the devil and then said, "Now you go. Heal the sick. Cast out demons. Preach the Kingdom. Walk in power." When I started to believe that, I stopped living on the defensive. I started walking like a son of God. So now when the enemy tries to whisper lies, I don't just panic. I speak truth. I declare who I am. I command every spirit of fear, lust, rage, addiction, or shame to leave. I don't entertain darkness. I evict it. Because this isn't a religion, it's a Kingdom. And the King gave me the keys.

Reflection Questions:

Do you truly believe you have authority in Christ?

Are there areas where you've given the enemy place instead of taking your place in victory?

What would change in your life if you began walking in your full spiritual authority?

Prayer:

Lord, thank You for the cross. Thank You for giving me authority—not because of who I am, but because of who You are. I receive the victory You purchased with Your blood. I take back every place I gave to the enemy, and I stand in my rightful position as a child of God. I declare freedom, power, and wholeness over my life. In Your name, Jesus. Amen.

NOTES

SET THE CAPTIVES FREE

Chapter 16

"The Spirit of the Lord God is upon Me, because the Lord has anointed Me to preach good tidings to the poor; He has sent Me to heal the brokenhearted, to proclaim liberty to the captives, and the opening of the prison to those who are bound." —Isaiah 61:1 (NKJV)

Before you can set others free, you need to be filled with the power of the Holy Spirit. Salvation seals you. Deliverance frees you. But the baptism of the Holy Spirit empowers you. Jesus didn't start His public ministry until after the Spirit descended on Him like a dove. And He told the disciples, "But you shall receive power when the Holy Spirit has come upon you; and you shall be witnesses to Me…" (Acts 1:8 NKJV).

That same power is what turns ordinary people into warriors. It's what gives your voice authority, your prayers fire, and your words weight in the spirit realm.

If you want to be a deliverer, you need more than just head knowledge—you need an encounter. You need to be filled. You need to be saturated in the presence of God. The devil doesn't fear church attendance. He fears believers filled with the Holy Ghost and walking in their God-given authority.

You have the authority because of the cross, but you walk in power because of the Spirit. This is why the enemy fights baptism in the Holy Spirit so hard. Because a believer who knows their identity, is filled with the Spirit, and walks in obedience is a threat to every stronghold in their city.

So, before we go further, if you haven't received the baptism of the Holy Spirit, ask Him now. Invite Him to fill you completely—not just with peace and comfort, but with power, boldness, and supernatural fire.

Now, let's talk about the call.

This book was never just about you. Yes, your freedom matters. Yes, your healing is important. But it doesn't end there. The same Jesus who said, "Come to Me" also said, "Go into all the world." If you've been set free, you're now called to help others get free. The Great Commission includes deliverance. Jesus said, "And these signs will follow those who believe: In My name they will cast out demons…" (Mark 16:17 NKJV). That's not just for pastors or evangelists.

That's for you.

You don't need a microphone. You don't need a platform. You just need to be willing. If the Holy Spirit lives inside of you, you carry the Kingdom. That means when you show up, freedom shows up. Light walks into the room. Chains start to break.

You might think, "But I'm not ready. I still have things to work through." GOOD. That means you're qualified. God doesn't use the perfect. He uses the surrendered.

Every scar you carry becomes a key to someone else's cell. Every wound you've let Him heal becomes a testimony of what's possible. When you say yes to being a deliverer, you become dangerous to Hell. Because you stop living just for yourself. You start moving with Heaven's mission. You start interrupting the devil's plans in other people's lives. You begin to speak the truth in dark places. You pray with authority. You confront lies. You cast out what doesn't belong.

Deliverance ministry is not about shouting at demons. It's about loving people enough to lead them into truth. It's about carrying the presence of God into the most broken places and watching Him do what only He can do. You were rescued for a reason. Don't waste your freedom. Use it.

SET THE CAPTIVES FREE.

Reflection Questions:

Have you asked for the baptism of the Holy Spirit and fire?

What has God set you free from that He may want to use to help others?

Are you willing to say yes to the call of being a deliverer?

Prayer:

Holy Spirit, I ask You to fill me completely. Baptize me with fire and power. I don't want to just be saved—I want to walk in authority. Use me to set captives free. Let my life be a weapon in Your hands. I say yes to Your call. Lead me, teach me, and send me. In Your name, Jesus. Amen.

NOTES

WALKING IN VICTORY

Chapter 17

"But thanks be to God, who gives us the victory through our Lord Jesus Christ." —1 Corinthians 15:57 (NKJV)

Seventeen chapters. That's not just a number—it's a prophetic declaration. Throughout the Bible, the number seventeen is associated with victory. On the 17th day of the second month, the flood came and wiped out the evil of the earth (Genesis 7:11). And on the 17th day of the seventh month, the ark rested on Mount Ararat—a place of deliverance and new beginnings (Genesis 8:4).

That's where you are now. You're not just coming to the end of a book. You're standing on your own Ararat. The flood has passed. The grave clothes are off. You are not who you were when you started this journey. You're no longer bound. No longer buried. You're walking in freedom. You're walking in victory.

But here's the truth: Victory is not just a feeling. It's a choice. A mindset. A way of life. God gave you free will. That means you get to choose what kind of life you walk in from here. You can go back to the familiar, or you can press forward into the fullness of your calling. You can be a survivor, or you can be a son or daughter. You can stay comfortable, or you can rise up as a warrior in the Kingdom of God. And let me tell you—it's worth it. Since walking with Jesus, I have seen real, undeniable victory. I am no longer addicted. I am no longer perverted. I am no longer angry, suicidal, or chained by shame. I have been made new.

But it didn't stop there. The fruit of freedom began to show up in every area of my life. I got out of prison, and within four years, I built a brand-new house. God has helped me start four businesses. I have become financially stable and well on my way to being able to provide for others, not just my own. I illustrated a children's book.

I wrote this book, something I once thought was impossible. I have a healthy, thriving marriage. I've learned to be a loving and present stepfather. I have a successful career. I've ministered in my workplaces, homeless shelters, jails, churches, malls, gas stations and the grocery stores. The same man who once ran the streets is now helping others walk in freedom.

That's victory. Victory means I no longer live under the weight of my past. I walk in authority. I speak the truth. I cast out demons. I heal the sick. I encourage the broken. I walk with purpose. I live as a son of God. And yet… I'm still growing, still learning, still becoming who God has called me to be. I don't claim to have it all figured out, but I'm hungry to keep learning. I want to understand His voice more clearly. I want to love more deeply. I want to lead more boldly. I want to keep becoming the man He destined me to be.

So, if you've made it to this point in the book, I want to say this: let's walk in victory together. Don't settle for surface-level Christianity. Don't stop at salvation. Keep going. Keep growing. Keep digging. The same Jesus who brought me out is calling you into a life of power, love, and purpose. You were not created to live bound. You were created to be free and to lead others into that same freedom. This isn't the end. It's the beginning.

Reflection Questions:

What victories has God already given you since coming to know Him?

What dreams or callings still feel too big for you—and how can you trust Him with them?

Are you willing to step fully into the identity, purpose, and victory God has called you to walk in?

Prayer:

Father, thank You for the victory I have in Jesus. Thank You for every stronghold broken, every chain destroyed, every lie exposed. Thank You for the freedom I now walk in—spirit, soul, and body. I choose surrender. I choose to walk in obedience, in truth, in power, and in love. Use my story to help others find their own breakthrough. Help me grow into everything You've created me to be. And let me never forget that this victory is not just for me. In Your name, Jesus. Amen.

NOTES

----

www.ingramcontent.com/pod-product-compliance
Lightning Source LLC
LaVergne TN
LVHW051240080426
835513LV00016B/1686